W9-ART-422

TOLEDO PUBLIC SCHOOLS
AUXILIARY SERVICES PROGRAM
FOR YEAR   **01/02**
TOLEDO CHRISTIAN SCHOOLS

Colin
Powell

Operations Desert Shield and Desert Storm tested the skills and talents that had earned General Colin Powell his brilliant military and political career. Powell is shown here in Saudi Arabia during Desert Shield.

JUNIOR ■ WORLD ■ BIOGRAPHIES

A JUNIOR *BLACK AMERICANS OF ACHIEVEMENT* BOOK

Colin Powell

MELISSA BANTA

CHELSEA JUNIORS

a division of CHELSEA HOUSE PUBLISHERS

English-language words that are italicized in the text can be found in the glossary at the back of the book.

Chelsea House Publishers

EDITORIAL DIRECTOR Richard Rennert
EXECUTIVE MANAGING EDITOR Karyn Gullen Browne
COPY CHIEF Robin James
PICTURE EDITOR Adrian G. Allen
ART DIRECTOR Robert Mitchell
MANUFACTURING DIRECTOR Gerald Levine

JUNIOR WORLD BIOGRAPHIES

SENIOR EDITOR Ann-Jeanette Campbell
SERIES DESIGN Marjorie Zaum

Staff for COLIN POWELL

COPY EDITOR Catherine Iannone
EDITORIAL ASSISTANT Kelsey Goss
PICTURE RESEARCHER Villette Harris
COVER ILLUSTRATION Cynthia Lechan

The Chelsea House World Wide Web site address is
http://www.chelseahouse.com

© 1995, 1998, 2001 by Chelsea House Publishers, a subsidiary of Haights Cross Communications. All rights reserved. Printed and bound in the United States of America.

7 9 8 6
Library of Congress Cataloging-in-Publication Data
Banta, Melissa.
       Colin Powell / Melissa Banta.
            p. cm.—(Junior world biographies)
       Includes bibliographical references (p.) and index.
ISBN 0-7910-1770-2.
       0-7910-2142-4 (PBK.)
    1. Powell, Colin L.—Juvenile literature. 2. Generals—United States—Biography—Juvenile literature. 3. Afro-American generals—Biography—Juvenile literature. 4. United States. Army—Biography—Juvenile literature.
[1. Powell, Colin L. 2. Generals. 3. Afro-Americans—Biography.] I. Title.II. Series.
E840.8.P68B36 1994
355'.0092—dc20
                                                                    94-8349
                                                                    CIP
                                                                    AC

Contents

On October 3, 1989, General Colin Powell formally became the chairman of the Joint Chiefs of Staff and received the congratulations of the outgoing chairman, Admiral William Crowe.

1

But You Can

In 1963, when Colin Luther Powell was a 26-year-old soldier, he went to a restaurant in Georgia to order a hamburger. The waitress asked him if he was a student from Africa. Powell replied no. Then the waitress asked him if he was from Puerto Rico. Powell again replied no. The waitress asked, "You're a Negro?" He said, "That's right." She said that she could not serve him a hamburger at the counter. He would have to go around to the back door of the restaurant to get it.

"All I wanted was a hamburger," Powell remembers. The following year, President Lyndon

B. Johnson signed into law the Civil Rights Act. One purpose of the law was to prohibit segregation, the policy that made some public places off-limits to blacks. After the law was passed, Powell returned to that restaurant counter in Georgia "and got my hamburger."

Powell has often encountered the racist belief that white people are superior to black people. But he has proven that through hard work and determination, it is possible to rise above the negative attitudes of others—far above them.

October 3, 1989, was one of the proudest days in Powell's life, and a day that made U.S. military history. On that day, Colin Powell officially accepted his new position as the 12th chairman of the Joint Chiefs of Staff (JCS) of the U.S. armed forces.

At age 52, Powell was not only the first black man to become chairman of the JCS, he was also the youngest. The JCS chairman is the principal military adviser to the president of the United States and the secretary of defense, as well as the leader of all four segments of the nation's armed forces. This includes the marine corps, army, navy, and air force.

As JCS chairman, Powell gave advice on whether to use military force in a given situation. When military action was taken, Powell helped determine how *troops* and weapons were used. Another important part of his job was to recommend to the president and Congress how much money the government should spend on defense and how large the military should be.

When President George Bush nominated Powell for chairman of the JCS, he gave him the highest recommendation. Noting Powell's distinguished career, the president said, "He's a complete soldier."

Standing more than six feet tall and weighing over 200 pounds, Powell looked proud and confident in his new role. "If a stranger had come into the room and been told that one person there was new to his job, he would never guess it was Powell," one government official observed. "The

9

Once Powell discovered the ROTC in college, he was on his way to the top military job in the country. Powell (right) reviews troops as the new chairman of the Joint Chiefs of Staff.

new chairman was utterly confident. He absolutely filled the room."

When Powell was a boy growing up in New York City, he did not have great ambitions. Few, if any, would have foreseen his future as one of the most powerful and respected leaders in the United States military. Throughout elementary school and high school, Colin felt little *motivation,* and he showed little interest in applying himself to his studies.

Then, at college, Powell signed up for the Reserve Officers' Training Corps (ROTC), a program that offers students military training and academic scholarships. He enjoyed it so much that he entered an ROTC summer training course at Fort Bragg, North Carolina.

Colin had grown up in racially mixed neighborhoods of New York City, and the ROTC mirrored those neighborhoods. He was unprepared for the racially segregated South. There, the young student-soldier came up against *Jim Crow laws.*

According to these laws, African Americans had to sit in separate sections of buses and theaters. They had to use designated drinking fountains and toilets. Blacks were not allowed to use public parks and beaches. The schools and hospitals that admitted blacks were never as good as those for whites.

Powell saw the *magnitude* of what he had to fight against if he wanted to get anywhere in this society. "For minority youth back in the mid- and late 1950s there were not that many avenues out. It was still a time when your possibilities were limited by your religious background or your racial heritage. I didn't understand that. It wasn't until I went into the army and was assigned to places like Fort Bragg, North Carolina, that I came to understand the nature of *bias*."

From this point on, Powell made up his mind to *excel* at whatever he did. He decided that he owed it to himself, and to the rest of his race, to better himself every way he could. The importance of education and hard work became clear to him, and Powell graduated from college at the top of his ROTC class, and with the highest rank, cadet colonel.

In 1962, Powell was sent to Southeast Asia to fight in the Vietnam War, where he won two medals for bravery. His Washington, D.C., career began in 1972 when he served as an *intern* at the White House. From then on, he shifted between political and military jobs, each step of the way earning great respect for his diplomatic and leadership skills. In 1989, he was promoted to four-star general.

In 1991, Powell went back to visit his old neighborhood in the South Bronx—now a depressed and troubled place. He gave a speech at Morris High School, where he had been a lackluster student. "I remember that front door," he told the students. "I remember the auditorium. I remember the feeling that you can't make it. But you can."

Powell had learned something since high school and he passed it on to his teenage audience: "Don't let your blackness be a problem to you. Let it be a problem to somebody else. Don't use it as an excuse for your own shortcomings. If you work hard success will come your way." The highest-ranking military officer in the United States then barked a command to his audience: "Stick with it. I'm giving you an order. Stick with it."

For Powell, the environment of the ROTC was both challenging and rewarding. His life became focused and he excelled in school as well as in the corps.

2

The Journey's Beginning

Colin Powell's parents were originally from Jamaica, an island in the Caribbean Sea. They met in New York City, where they both lived after moving to the United States in the 1920s. Luther Theopolis Powell, his father, came from a peasant farming family. He was the first in his family to come to America, and over time he brought other family members to join him. Maud Ariel McKoy, who would become Luther's wife, was the first child to be reunited with her mother, who had left

Jamaica earlier looking for work. In 1929, Luther and Maud were married.

Colin was born on April 5, 1937, in New York City. Marilyn, Colin's sister, was five and a half years old at the time. The family lived in Harlem, a large black community in the upper part of Manhattan in New York City. When Colin's parents had first moved there, during the Harlem *renaissance*, the neighborhood was a bustling artistic center for black culture, particularly attracting writers and musicians.

By the 1930s, however, Harlem began to suffer urban decline. It was the decade of the Great Depression, when across the country, money and food were scarce. Businesses closed, and many people lost their jobs. Harlem felt the pinch as much as everywhere else.

In 1940, when Colin was three, the family moved to Kelly Street in the South Bronx—the "beautiful Bronx" as it was known then—just across the Harlem River. Hunts Point, Powell's Bronx neighborhood, has since become one of the most crime-ridden, dangerous spots of any city in the United States. Drugs, drinking, and street gangs threatened the neighborhood back then, too. "But it was nowhere near as bad as it later became," Powell recalled.

"What many people now call a slum was . . . a neat place to grow up when I was a boy," Powell said of his old neighborhood. "Our favorite pastime was 'making the walk.' Every block along 163rd had a repeating pattern to it. There was always a Jewish bakery, a Puerto Rican grocery, a Jewish candy store, a Chinese laundry, and other specialty stores." "Making the walk" meant covering the neighborhood's territory on foot with friends, watching, listening, talking, and goofing around. On Saturdays, Colin and his friends would spend hours at the Tiffany Theater where they watched B-grade westerns.

Colin's favorite hobbies included playing stickball and flying kites from rooftops. He and his friends made their own games too. They made openings of various sizes in cigar boxes and tossed marbles in them, and they played checkers with bottle caps they had filled with wax.

Powell remembered, "Almost all of my aunts and uncles lived on Kelly Street. We were a close-knit family that cared very much about each other." His sister, Marilyn, who grew up to become a teacher, also remembers how "the neighborhood was like a small town. Everybody looked out for each other. We could never get into trouble. Everywhere you went there were 40 pairs of eyes watching you."

Luther and Maud Powell provided a very close, loving, and structured home for their children and did their best to instill self-confidence in them. They were active in the Church of England in Jamaica and later the Episcopal church in New York, and their religious devotion provided a strong foundation for the family. Colin sometimes participated in services as an altar attendant.

In Colin's neighborhood, "everybody was a minority." Many ethnic groups, including African, Irish, Italian, Polish, and Puerto Rican, lived there together, so Colin did not grow up with the notion of a separate privileged majority. "I never thought there was something wrong with me because I was black."

The neighborhood in which Colin (second from right) grew up was home to families of several different races and ethnic backgrounds. Colin's friends remember that they did not have to go out for ethnic food—they could simply have dinner at the home of one of their pals.

In their homeland of Jamaica, Colin's parents had not experienced racism the same way that blacks living in America had. West Indian blacks were descended from slaves too, but the conditions of slavery on the islands were very different from those of American slavery. These differences had an impact on how the descendants of slaves saw themselves.

In the West Indies, slaves were not fed by their masters. They farmed plots of land to feed themselves and sold the extra produce in the marketplace. Also, slavery was abolished earlier in the British-owned West Indies than in the United States. The British then integrated the black population into its business and educational systems. These factors helped create a black self-image that was less *brutalized* than that of African Americans and made it easier for children to grow up with pride and dignity.

Although Luther and Maud Powell did not finish high school themselves, they stressed the importance of education to their children. Books filled their house. They told Colin and his sister, Marilyn, to "strive for a good education. Make something of your life."

Powell's parents also taught their children the value of hard work. Luther worked in a garment factory as a shipping clerk, and Maud worked at home as a seamstress. They both spent long, hard hours at their jobs and were committed to doing their very best.

According to Powell, learning his parents' lessons in life "wasn't a matter of spending a great deal of time with my parents discussing things. It was just the way they lived their lives." Through their love and sacrifice, Colin's parents passed on their family values. "You realized that these modestly educated immigrants were not doing all of this for themselves; they were doing all of this for you," Powell said. "So it was unthinkable in the family not do something," not to make something of yourself.

The Powell family at sister Marilyn's college graduation in 1952: (from left to right) Luther, Marilyn, Maud, and Colin.

The Powells' extended family was full of success stories. Through education and hard work, several of Colin's cousins had become lawyers, businesspeople, or psychologists, and one was an ambassador. While Colin may be the most stunning success in his family, he did not start out that way.

Colin attended public school, but he did not do well in his classes. Once when he was eight years old, Colin played hooky. When he returned home too early, a neighbor spotted him. His parents decided that for the next few days, an adult would take the young boy all the way to the classroom door. They were serious about their son getting an education, but Colin still was not very enthusiastic.

"I was the one who was always asking our mother to read street signs to me and spell words when I was little when she was taking me out for a walk," Powell's sister, Marilyn, remembers. "Colin could not have cared less. But look at us now. I guess he was a late bloomer."

In fifth grade, Colin was placed in a special class for slow students, and he admits that in both his junior and senior high schools he "horsed around a lot." Back then, Intermediate School 52 and Morris High School had serious problems with drugs, violence, and bad dropout rates, but not to the extent they did later, when such problems made headline news.

Colin had wanted to attend the Bronx High School of Science, one of the best high schools in the country, but his grades were too low. Instead, he went to Morris High School, where he earned C grades. A fellow student remembers him as "an average, do-the-right-thing kind of guy."

Outside of classes, Powell made more of an impact. Beginning to show his knack for leadership, he was elected class representative. The Service League, a committee of students who helped with various chores at the school, elected him treasurer. Colin also participated briefly in sports.

A tall, strong teenager, he got a job working part-time in a baby furniture store. Like his parents, he worked long hours for little pay, and he continued there until his second year of college.

In 1954, Colin graduated from high school. He had applied to the City College of New York (CCNY) and New York University (NYU) and was accepted at both schools—remarkable considering his *mediocre* academic performance. Powell remembers making the decision between the two schools fairly easily: "NYU cost $750 a year; CCNY cost $10. That was the end of that."

At CCNY, Powell took courses in *engineering* but later switched to geology, the study of the earth, which he thought would be easier. His grades did not show improvement. Then one day, the sight of the army's Reserve Officers' Training Corps members on campus caught Colin's attention. Impressed by the uniforms of the Pershing Rifles drill team, one of the more dedicated units within the ROTC, he decided to enroll in the program. "The Pershing Rifles were the ones who walked around with a little whipped cord on their shoulders, suggesting that they were a little more serious than the average ROTC cadet," Powell remembers. "That appealed to me."

The ROTC program enabled college students to get military training and become an officer in the armed services. Colin thought it would be an opportunity for some excitement. He assumed he would stay in the army for a few years "and then come home and get a real job." He never dreamed he would make the army his career.

The discipline, physical activity, and *camaraderie* of military life suited Powell well. The young cadet enjoyed his friendships with fellow ROTC members. Colin became the leader of the Pershing Rifles and inspired his ROTC classmates to work their hardest. In his senior year, Colin became a cadet colonel, the ROTC's highest rank.

A fellow Pershing Rifleman remembers, "Even back then he had the stamina. He had that bearing. Even in the cadets he was very stern, very disciplined, very military-oriented. But he had a good personality too; he was one of the guys."

When he graduated in 1958, Powell was at the top of his ROTC class. Then he had a *revelation:* "I realized . . . this is fun and you do it well." Powell had found his calling in life.

Major Colin Powell on his second tour of duty in Vietnam, 1968 to 1969. While he was fighting for his country abroad, racial violence threatened his family's safety at home.

3
Those Who
Went Before

After graduating from college, Powell became a second lieutenant in the army, earning $60 a week. The army Powell joined was an integrated one, in which blacks and whites served side by side in the same units. It had not always been that way.

Powell realized time and again that he would not have been able to reach the powerful position in the military that he eventually did "without the sacrifices of those of our soldiers who served this great nation in war for 300 years previously. All is on the backs and the contributions of those who went before me."

"Going back to the early colonies, blacks have willingly served in the military in times of foreign and domestic danger," Powell stated at a lecture on the history of blacks in the military. "During most of that history, they would only be allowed to serve when there was dying to be done. It was only after the Civil War that black units were allowed to remain on active duty in the absence of a war. And only in the last 30 years, in my generation, did we achieve full integration and full opportunity."

Until recently, blacks in the army were subject to the same kind of *discrimination* they suffered in civilian society, receiving menial jobs, low pay, and substandard education. Blacks were usually limited to positions as laborers, cooks, or any job that did not involve the use of weapons. They commonly received only half the pay of white soldiers. If they did enter combat, they often had inferior training and weapons.

Before the American Revolution, blacks were kept out of the militia unless they were needed in an emergency to combat Native Americans. Whites feared that if blacks had guns, they might use them against whites. At the time of the American Revolution, George Washington prohibited blacks from fighting in his Continental army—until the British started recruiting them. Then he grudgingly let them in. About 5,000 blacks served in the army, mostly in menial tasks.

During the Civil War, Lincoln forbade the recruitment of blacks in order to avoid racial tension in the Union army. Manpower was desperately needed, however, and Northern generals formed black regiments without permission. Lincoln finally relented, and of the 185,000 black soldiers recruited, 38,000 died in the Civil War.

After the Civil War, the 24th and 25th Infantry and the 9th and 10th Cavalry were made permanent and stationed on the frontier, where they would not be noticed. The Native Americans dubbed them Buffalo Soldiers because the curly hair and stamina of the soldiers reminded them of the prized animal of the American West.

(While attending army college at the fort where the 10th Cavalry had been stationed, Powell discovered that the only mention of this unit was a sign that read Buffalo Soldier Alley. His predecessors deserved greater recognition than that, and so he suggested building a monument in their honor. Eight years later, Powell attended the groundbreaking ceremony, and today there stands an impressive statue of a Buffalo Soldier on horseback.)

The road to equality and justice for blacks in the military had its high points and low points. In 1879, Henry Flipper became the first African American to graduate from the United States Military Academy at West Point, the premier military school in the country. Just 27 years later, however, a riot erupted in Texas, where the 25th Infantry was stationed. One hundred sixty-seven black soldiers, some with more than 25 years of service, were dishonorably discharged without any evidence to convict them.

In the First World War, little progress was made, and about 370,000 black soldiers were treated with discrimination. The world changed more quickly after World War I, and by the time the United States entered World War II, there were black combat units and officer candidate schools as well as training for black combat pilots. Benjamin O. Davis, Sr., had become the first black general in the army.

Henry Ossian Flipper was the first African American to graduate from West Point. Later, he was charged with embezzlement. Found innocent, he was still dishonorably discharged from the army.

Benjamin O. Davis, Sr. (above), was the first black
general in the army. His son, Benjamin O. Davis, Jr.
(below), was the first black general in the air force.

34

In 1948, President Harry S. Truman ordered the armed forces to end segregation of blacks and whites and to institute the policies of fair employment. Although it was very unpopular at the time (much as the issues of women in combat and homosexuals in the military have since been), it proved to be a sound decision. With integration, black soldiers would have the same tasks and responsibilities as white soldiers, with the same pay and possibilities for advancement. At last, blacks serving in the military could feel they truly belonged. They could now gain the respect due them from the country for which they had always been willing to fight.

Colin Powell never forgot that his own success was the product of years of struggle by those who came before him. After Powell achieved nationwide fame, a black waiter recognized him in a restaurant one day and approached him. "General . . . ," he said, "I just wanted to thank you and say it's been good to see you here. I was in World War II, and I fought all the way from North Africa to Italy." Powell respectfully replied, "Brother, I ought to be thanking you."

When Powell entered the army full-time in 1958, he was sent to Fort Benning, Georgia, for basic training. His first assignment was in West Germany, where he rose to the rank of first lieutenant. When Powell returned to the United States at age 24, he became battalion adjutant—an assistant to a commander of hundreds of soldiers—in Fort Devens, Massachusetts. Ordinarily a higher-ranking officer was appointed to this position (usually a captain), so even at this early stage of Powell's career, someone in the army recognized his exceptional talents.

Powell found he could communicate comfortably with both his superiors and his troops, and he was well liked by both. Because he had once been an underachiever himself, he understood how to motivate soldiers who needed discipline or who had low morale.

In 1962, Powell met Alma Johnson, a young woman from Birmingham, Alabama, on a blind date. The daughter of a high school principal, Alma worked as a *speech pathologist.* "He was absolutely the nicest person I had ever met," Alma remembers thinking. Over the next few months they fell in love, and by August of that same year they were married.

The newly married couple soon had to part, however, because Powell was given an assignment overseas. Powell joined the U.S. military forces in Vietnam, where he served as an adviser to a South Vietnam infantry battalion. Since the 1950s, the United States had been involved in supporting the South Vietnamese government in a civil war against Vietnamese Communists. In the early 1960s, President John F. Kennedy increased the number of U.S. military forces there as tensions between North and South Vietnam grew.

One day while Powell was patrolling the North Vietnamese border, he stepped on a punji-stick trap——a sharp stake hidden under the water of a rice paddy. The stake went right through his foot. The army sent him to a nearby hospital where his wound was treated. He received a Purple Heart, a medal awarded to servicemen wounded in combat.

In another mission, Powell was on board a helicopter when it crashed in the Vietnamese jungle. Although he had broken his ankle in the crash, he managed to rescue the other soldiers from the burning wreckage. He received the Soldier's Medal, awarded for risking one's life in a noncombat situation.

Back in the United States, Alma had given birth to their first child, Michael. He was two weeks old before news of his birth reached his father in Vietnam. It would be more than a year and a half before Powell could return home to see his baby boy.

While Powell fought in Vietnam, Alma lived in Birmingham, Alabama, with her parents. Like many other American cities at the time, Birmingham was burning with racial tension. In May 1963, Martin Luther King, Jr., and other African-American leaders organized a nonviolent demon-

Powell was awarded the Soldier's Medal for dragging injured soldiers from the wreckage of this helicopter. He had broken his own ankle in the crash.

stration in Birmingham to protest discrimination against blacks.

Under orders from city leaders to break up the demonstration, the police attacked the crowds with clubs and specially trained German shepherd dogs. Firemen sprayed men and women with high-pressure water hoses, knocking them down with terrible force. No one stopped the white authorities from brutally beating the demonstrators.

When Powell came home to visit his family for Christmas, he was shocked by the violent racial conflict in the States. He was risking his life fighting for his country thousands of miles away in Vietnam, while his own people were neither safe nor protected at home. "I was hit full force with what had happened in my absence," he recalls. "I was stunned, disheartened, and angry." Powell became more committed than ever to the civil rights movement.

In 1968, Powell asked for and received permission to enroll in the army's Command and General Staff College at Fort Leavenworth, Kansas. Ever mindful of his parents' belief in the value of education, Powell also applied for permission to get a master's degree in geology at a civilian school. His supervisors turned down this request. The officer in charge simply said, "Your college record isn't good enough." This rejection made Powell angry. He tried to do his very best at Leavenworth to prove himself, and he graduated second out of 1,244 students.

After graduating, he was sent back to Vietnam. By 1968, the United States had boosted its military force to more than 500,000. In spite of this, the American military could not win the war or bring it to a satisfactory end.

Powell saw constant combat in Vietnam. Then one day, he was unexpectedly taken out of action and promoted to the division's assistant chief of staff. The commander of the 23rd Infantry had read an article in the *Army Times* newspaper about the top five students of the recent graduating class at Leavenworth. "I've got the number two Leavenworth graduate in my division, and he's stuck in the boonies?" he said. "I want him on my staff."

When he first entered the army, Powell had been told it would take 20 years to reach the rank of lieutenant colonel. "I was told, 'If you do everything well and keep your nose clean for 20 years, we'll make you a lieutenant colonel.' That was my goal," Powell remembers. Powell made lieutenant colonel in only 12 years.

Powell frequently welcomed and met with foreign dignitaries. Here he welcomes General Mikhail A. Moiseyev, his counterpart in the former Soviet Union.

4

Rules
To Live By

Upon his return home from Vietnam in 1969, Powell got his wish to go to graduate school. He was granted permission to attend George Washington University in Washington, D.C., where he enrolled in the master of business administration (M.B.A.) program. He reasoned that "good business managers are needed in the Department of the Defense." He received his degree in 1971.

The following year, another welcome opportunity came Powell's way. One day he received a telephone call from a top army official. "Colin," the official said, "the Infantry Branch wants one of its people to become a White House Fellow. We want you to apply." White House Fellows work for one year as interns in various departments of the *executive* branch of the government. The fellowship provides young career men and women with firsthand experience in government policy making. Not only is a fellowship an honor and a remarkable education in the way the federal government is run, but the Fellows meet powerful Washingtonians and are frequently given important job opportunities.

Out of 1,500 applicants, Powell and 16 others passed round after round of selection—beginning with an eight-page application form and ending with a nonstop weekend interview—to receive a fellowship in 1972.

Powell was assigned to the Office of Management and Budget (OMB), which oversees what happens to the government's money. The OMB director was Caspar W. Weinberger and his deputy was Frank Carlucci, both of whom would later serve as secretaries of defense and would be important figures in Powell's career. At the OMB, Powell learned a great deal about financial planning at the highest levels of management.

When the fellowship year was over, Powell wanted a battalion commander's assignment. The only immediate opening was in South Korea, but he would have to leave his family—which by now also included two daughters, Linda and Annemarie—behind. The battalion that Powell was placed in charge of in the Republic of Korea was a mess. It was riddled with racial tension, drug abuse, and low morale, and the troops lacked discipline.

Powell was forceful but encouraging in addressing the outfit's problems. He worked his troops so hard that they had little time or energy for drugs and troublemaking. "We ran them four miles every morning, and by night they were too tired to get into trouble," Powell said. Powell instilled in his soldiers a sense of duty and enthu-

After his first taste of politics in Washington, Powell requested a field command and was sent to South Korea. There he proved to be an exemplary leader.

siasm, and before long the battalion showed discipline and the ability to work with one another. According to Powell's commanding officer, General Hank "Gunfighter" Emerson, the Second Infantry was "a good place to test your commanders, and Powell was out ———— standing."

Powell was once described as a "tough-asnails military man" with "compassion and soul." He required a lot from his troops, but he also showed great understanding and fairness toward them. To Powell, the army was like a family—both demanding and supportive.

In 1975–76, Powell attended the National War College and graduated with distinction. Powell's next job was as executive to the special assistant to the secretary and deputy secretary of defense in President Jimmy Carter's administration. It was the first of Powell's many advisory positions that combined and enhanced his military and political skills. In 1979, Powell earned his first general's star.

When Ronald Reagan became president in 1980, he appointed Powell's old bosses Weinberger and Carlucci as defense secretary and deputy defense secretary, respectively. Powell had made a good impression on them when they worked together at the OMB, and they hired him. Powell first served as Carlucci's assistant during the transition between the Carter and Reagan administrations. Then in 1983, he returned as Weinberger's senior military assistant, after a stint in the field as an army commander.

In the Defense Department, Powell's day usually began at 6:30 in the morning, and he did not finish until 7:00 at night. He worked well with others, both above and below him, and earned a reputation as someone who could get a job done quickly. Powell put his ability to work with people to good use. One of his most valued skills was the ability to run a successful meeting. He made sure that everyone was listened to and got a chance to have their say, then summarized the important points before adjourning.

Secretary Weinberger had high praise for his assistant. "He has excelled in everything he has touched as he always will," Weinberger said. "I don't think you can find anyone who has anything bad to say about Colin Powell, which is an extraordinary thing when you've been around Washington as long as he has—in highly sensitive and vital assignments."

Although his title was assistant, Powell's responsibilities were greater than most soldiers or politicians would ever carry. Before long, he was promoted to a two-star major general. The powerful team of Weinberger and Powell worked closely together, traveling to more than 35 countries, meeting with foreign military officials, and handling many complex assignments, including the U.S. invasion of Grenada, a tiny island in the Caribbean Sea.

In 1983, revolutionaries in Grenada arrested the island's prime minister and set up a new government. President Reagan ordered 1,900 U.S. troops to overthrow the government, claiming that the rebels' connection to Communist Cuba and the Soviet Union threatened American interests and put American students living on the island in danger. Powell kept the White House informed about the Defense Department's plans and gave updates during the course of the mission. The invasion was over in less than one week and was deemed a success by the White House.

Powell preferred fieldwork "close to the troops" to a desk job, and in 1986 he became commander of the U.S. Army V Corps in Frankfurt, West Germany. Promoted to lieutenant general (a three-star general), he was in charge of more than 72,000 troops. Powell felt he was "probably the happiest general in the world."

But the general would not stay in the field for long. Six months after he received his new command, he was asked to return to Washington. Carlucci had just been appointed head of the National Security Council (NSC), probably one of the toughest possible assignments at the time, and he needed someone with Powell's *savoir faire* to be his deputy in the White House.

The NSC's reputation had been shattered by the Iran-contra scandal, which broke in November 1986. It was the biggest scandal to hit the U.S. government since Watergate. The NSC includes four prominent members: the president, the vice president, the secretary of defense, and the secretary of state. The council's leader is

Frank Carlucci first worked with Powell at the Office of Management and Budget. Subsequently Carlucci recommended Powell for many high-level government positions.

the national security adviser and his assistant is the deputy. Beyond those members, there is a large staff of support personnel. The NSC's job is to advise the president on defense and foreign policy issues. The Iran-contra scandal involved NSC members secretly taking matters into their own hands, disregarding presidential policies, and breaking the law in the process.

Some members of the NSC had participated in selling weapons to the Middle Eastern country of Iran—not only for money but in exchange for the release of American hostages. There were three primary infractions:

First: At the time, Iran was at war with its neighbor Iraq, and President Reagan had said that the United States would not assist Iran in this war.

Second: American hostages were being held by a group of Iranian terrorists. The guns-for-hostages deal violated the president's policy that the United States would not bargain with terrorists.

Third: In a final twist to the story, members of the NSC took part of the money they made selling the weapons to Iran and used it to help contra rebels in Nicaragua. The contras had long been fighting to take over the Nicaraguan government. The question of U.S. aid and involvement had already been settled in Congress: in 1984, Congress passed a law that prohibited U.S. military aid to the contras.

Once news of the Iran-contra affair broke, it became a national scandal. Powell had sensed that something was wrong in 1985 when he was

Weinberger's senior military assistant. At first, he had simply been asked for information and prices on weaponry, which he provided in a routine manner. By the time he and Weinberger discovered what the NSC was doing, John Poindexter, the head of the NSC, had persuaded President Reagan to approve the sale of arms in exchange for the hostages' release.

It was Powell's job to help deliver missiles to Iran, but he obeyed the orders reluctantly. He wrote a memo to Poindexter, reminding him that by law Congress had to be notified of certain types of arms sales. His memo was ignored.

"His whole conduct during that time was *impeccable,*" Weinberger said of Powell. It was much more than could be said of virtually everyone else involved in the scandal.

Carlucci now called on Powell to become his deputy in the NSC because he needed a strong, reliable leader. He could not, however, convince Powell to accept the job. A request from the president was needed.

The phone call came. "I know you've been looking forward to this command," said President Reagan, referring to Powell's post in Germany, "but we need you here." Powell replied, "Mr. President, I'm a soldier and if I can help, I'll come."

Powell began his new job back in Washington in 1987. He worked closely with Carlucci to restructure the NSC. In response to the Iran-contra affair, Powell set in place a watchful *chain of command* to prevent anything like it from happening again.

Carlucci trusted his deputy and sometimes asked Powell to represent him in the daily security briefings with President Reagan. Reagan liked Powell and the two men worked well together, as Carlucci had hoped.

Later that year, Weinberger resigned as defense secretary and Carlucci took his place. Powell was the logical choice to replace Carlucci as national security adviser. He had successfully restored confidence in the NSC, he knew the inner workings of the organization, and he had the confidence of the president of the United States.

As national security adviser, Powell's days still began at 6:30 in the morning, when he arrived in the office to study military and political reports. At 7:00 A.M., he met with the secretaries of state and defense. A few hours later, he met with the president for the daily briefing.

"It was a heck of a homework quiz," Powell said. "I would give him a warning of what was coming our way, or sometimes just philosophize: for example, what was happening in the Soviet Union or how Congress was reacting to a particular issue. It was a challenge, but it becomes a natural one because you're doing it every day."

Powell took part in planning the superpower summit meetings between President Reagan and Mikhail Gorbachev, then the leader of the former Soviet Union. Powell received a Distinguished Service Medal for his work on a U.S.–Soviet weapons reduction agreement.

For the first time, Powell was a public figure who had to face reporters. According to him, as a White House official, "you'd better have a lot of information. You cannot be wrong. If you're wrong, you're a headline." In spite of his annoyance with the press—"All they ever want to know is who did what to whom"—Powell became a respected and effective spokesperson for the NSC.

As national security adviser, Powell had daily meetings with President Ronald Reagan to discuss current events.

As Powell's responsibilities grew, he relied on a simple set of rules by which to live and work. They included the following:

- It is not as bad as you think. It will look better in the morning.
- Get mad, then get over it.
- You cannot make someone else's choices. You should not let someone else make yours.
- Be careful what you choose. You might get it.
- Check small things.
- Share credit.
- Remain calm. Be kind.
- Have a vision. Be demanding.
- It can be done.

One of the most important responsibilities Powell had during Desert Shield and Desert Storm was to hold briefings where he explained the operations to reporters.

5

Persian
Gulf Crisis

President Reagan's successor, George Bush, wanted to appoint his own NSC adviser, so Powell and Reagan left the White House together. Before they did, however, the president promoted his trusty adviser. Powell was now one of only 10 four-star generals in the country.

The army appointed Powell the commander in chief of the U.S. Forces Command. He supervised all army ground forces in the United States, which included more than 250,000 active-duty soldiers and 300,000 reserves.

Not long after, Dick Cheney, President Bush's new secretary of defense, called Powell. "I have recommended that the president appoint you [to the position of chairman of the Joint Chiefs of Staff]," Cheney said. "He has accepted my recommendation." Powell became the JCS chairman on October 3, 1989. He was the highest-ranking military official in the country, overseeing the army, air force, navy, and marine corps.

While some officials felt that he lacked sufficient combat experience for the job, Powell had proven that he was a good commander who could communicate with heads of state as well as soldiers in the field. His leadership skills, his experience in foreign policy, and his high moral standards made him the president's first choice. The Senate unanimously approved his appointment.

Two big international crises hit Powell's desk, one right after the other. To make the military decisions they demanded, Powell had to weigh many concerns. He had always believed that military force should be used only if necessary and that if soldiers had to fight, it should be for a just cause. Not only did he think about political losses and gains, but personal ones too. He knew the pain a family feels when a soldier is injured or dies. He would have to decide whether to put soldiers at that risk. In the wake of the Vietnam War, Powell was determined "that our forces remain strong, that they always have what is needed to accomplish their mission, that they are never asked to respond to the call of an uncertain trumpet."

The Vietnam War had been very unpopular. The military effort was halfhearted, and many American citizens publicly and actively protested the United States's involvement. News of the ever-increasing number of dead and wounded soldiers and those missing in action was devastating, and in spite of its sophisticated weaponry, the United States failed to win the war. Powell condensed the Vietnam experience into a clear-cut military code: "Strike suddenly, decisively, and in sufficient force to resolve the matter," he said. "Do it quickly; and do it with a minimum loss of life." If these conditions could not be met, any military action would be courting disaster.

In Central America, General Manuel Noriega, the dictator of Panama, had been deeply involved in international drug smuggling. For many years he had had a working relationship with the CIA, but by late 1989, the relationship had soured and President Bush wanted to remove Noriega from power. Powell preferred trying to negotiate with him. When Noriega's troops killed a U.S. marine, however, Powell changed his mind.

With General Maxwell R. Thurman, Powell planned Operation Just Cause. It began on December 20, 1989, when, in the words of General Powell, "18,000 teenagers with guns" were sent to invade Panama and capture Noriega. "We will chase him and we will find him," said Powell. The operation was a quick, full-scale strike. Noriega was captured and brought to the United States. He was tried in a court of law and found guilty of charges of drug trafficking.

Less than one year later, in August 1990, the White House received news that 80,000 Iraqi troops led by President Saddam Hussein had invaded Kuwait, an adjoining country. The invasion gave Iraq control over Kuwait's oil fields and put Iraqi troops in a position to attack Saudi Arabia. Hussein's actions caused an uproar because the international community and world economy rely heavily on oil from that region.

As a first response, the United Nations (UN) imposed *economic sanctions,* prohibiting trade with Iraq. Powell favored these sanctions over military force. President Bush, however, wanted more. He asked Powell to create a special American military presence in the area. The plan became known as Operation Desert Shield. Within a few months, more than 180,000 U.S. troops were sent to Saudi Arabia.

These soldiers and the UN's economic sanctions seemed to have little effect on Hussein, whose troops remained in Kuwait. In November,

Bush ordered twice as many troops sent to the Persian Gulf area.

Powell believed that like Vietnam, a war against Iraq would become unpopular. He feared that too many American men and women would die and that faith in the U.S. military—both internally and externally—would *deteriorate*. He urged President Bush to rely on economic sanctions.

"I don't think there's time," Bush told Powell. So, although Powell disagreed with the president's plan, he followed his commander in chief's orders. "My job is to make sure that if it is necessary to go to war, we go to war to win," he said.

Powell first spent time studying the history of that area of the Middle East. "I always like to have a context for what I do," he said, "so I know I'm in the right stadium and I'm playing the right game. Then I can go on the field and play it. History helps put me in that context."

He then began the buildup of troops, tanks, ships, and aircraft in the Persian Gulf. It took two months to transform Operation Desert Shield, a defensive force, into Operation Desert Storm, an offensive force. The mission: attack Iraq's 1-million-man army.

Meanwhile the UN's security council gave Hussein until January 15, 1991, to remove his troops from Kuwait. Otherwise, it stated, "all necessary means" would be used to drive them out. More than 18 nations agreed to contribute forces to the effort. Powell devised a well-designed plan under which these multinational forces from Europe and the Middle East could work.

Powell addresses the crew of the USS Wisconsin *in the Persian Gulf. The battleship was part of the increase of force during Desert Shield.*

The January 15 deadline passed. Hussein still had not withdrawn his forces. On January 17, early in the morning, allied forces led by the United States began a massive assault against Iraqi troops and military targets from the air. More than 1,000 missions took place in the first days, making it the largest air strike in history. By this time, more than 500,000 U.S. troops were stationed in the gulf region.

During the first week of the war, Powell stayed in his Washington office around the clock in order to supervise the relentless air strike. Powell planned to isolate "the brains of the operation" and then cut off Iraqi soldiers from goods and ammunition.

A little over a month later, Iraq's military communications systems no longer functioned. Iraqi forces suffered many losses. On February 24, the allied troops attacked for the first time on the ground, routing the Iraqi army. Soon afterward, Hussein said he would withdraw from Kuwait and meet the demands laid out by the UN.

Powell played a vital role in communications among White House officials, military leaders, and members of Congress during the war. For example, Powell worked together with General H. Norman Schwarzkopf, who was head of the U.S. Central Command in Saudi Arabia, to develop detailed strategies for Operation Desert Storm. Powell then reported the details of the plan to the president and Congress.

Practicing one of his rules to live by, Powell gave thanks to his troops for the operation's success. "Wherever I go, people want to shake my hand and pat me on the back," he said to them. "But it's your hand they want to shake and your back they want to pat."

After Operation Desert Storm, Powell and the soldiers were national heroes. Some government officials recommended that he, along with General Schwarzkopf, be given a fifth general's star. Powell, now a favorite subject of the press, claimed to be unhappy with all the attention. "I can't tell you how much I hate this," he said. "I don't control my life anymore." Some, however, argue that Powell is fully in control and that he is a master at using the media to promote himself.

With the Persian Gulf War over, Powell took some time at home away from the crowds and the press. He worked on his favorite hobby, fixing Volvo cars, and spent time with his wife, Alma, and their three grown children. Powell's father died in 1978 at age 80, and his mother died in 1984 at age 82. Nevertheless, "My parents are a very real presence for me," Powell once said. "They are in the house whenever I move. They haven't left my life."

Powell left the post of chairman of the JCS in the fall of 1993. Aside from the Noriega affair and the Persian Gulf War, he had monitored the strained relations between the United States and Iraq. He had studied the breakdown of the Soviet Union and the economic and social instability in Eastern Europe. And he had paid close attention to the devastating and brutal war among Serbs, Croats, and Muslims in the former Yugoslavia.

Defense Secretary Dick Cheney confers with Powell as they testify before the Senate regarding the Persian Gulf War. Three days later, allied ground forces attacked Iraq.

Domestically, his concerns focused on economics. In order to slow the increase in the national debt, the hundreds of billions of dollars the U.S. government has borrowed, the defense budget had to be reduced. Powell worked with the Defense Department to trim military spending and to plan the closing of military bases.

Throughout this process, Powell had to remain true to his fundamental belief that the military must maintain a strong force in order to be

President Bill Clinton congratulates Powell and his wife, Alma, upon Powell's retirement as chairman of the Joint Chiefs of Staff in September 1993. Many people would like to see Powell run for president himself one day.

able to take action whenever there may be a crisis that calls for military aid. "Peace through strength vanishes as a possibility if there is no strength," he explained.

When General Powell retired from the JCS chairmanship, many people had different ideas of what he should do. Many former government officials earn a lot of money making speeches and writing books. Top private corporations want people like Powell on their boards or as their directors. Other possibilities include becoming the director of the CIA or FBI, the secretary of defense, or the secretary of state. Perhaps, like General (and President) Eisenhower, Powell would become the president of a major university.

Many would like to see Powell become president or vice president of the United States. When asked, however, his standard comment has been, "I have no interest in politics at the moment."

To young people of all races, Colin Powell has become a role model. "There are no secrets to success," he once told a group of students. "Success is the result of perfection, hard work, learning from failure, loyalty to those for whom you work, and persistence. You must be ready for opportunity when it comes."

Further Reading

Binkin, Martin, and Mark J. Eitelberg. *Blacks and the Military.* Washington, D.C.: Brookings Institution, 1982.

Brown, Warren. *Colin Powell.* New York: Chelsea House, 1992.

Haskins, James. *Count Your Way Through the Arab World.* Minneapolis: Carolrhoda Books, 1991.

Landau, Elaine. *Colin Powell: Four Star General.* New York: Franklin Watts, 1991.

Lawson, Don. *The War in Vietnam.* New York: Franklin Watts, 1981.

Leckie, William H. *The Buffalo Soldiers: A Narrative of the Negro Cavalry in the West.* Norman: University of Oklahoma Press, 1985.

Glossary

bias   a strong feeling for or against without enough reason; prejudice

brutalized   treated cruelly or harshly

camaraderie   a spirit of friendliness or togetherness

chain of command   a series of executive positions in order of power

deteriorate   to become weakened in quality or condition

discrimination   the act of treating some people better than others because of bias or prejudice

economic sanctions   restrictions placed on the trade or commerce of a country that has broken an international law or agreement, designed to encourage change in the country's behavior

engineering   the use of scientific knowledge for practical purposes, such as designing and building bridges, roads, and tunnels

excel   to do better than others

executive having responsibility for management or administration

impeccable absolutely clear of any fault or guilt

intern a student in a professional field gaining supervised experience

Jim Crow laws slang term for laws and customs that segregated blacks and whites

magnitude of great size, importance or significance

mediocre neither good nor bad; ordinary

motivation the need or desire to perform an action

renaissance rebirth or revival; a period of intense interest in culture and the arts

revelation a startling, clear discovery of truth

savoir faire a knowledge of how to behave appropriately

speech pathologist one who studies or helps to correct abnormal speech patterns

troops soldiers, or a group of soldiers

Chronology

1937   Born Colin Luther Powell on April 5 in the Harlem district of New York City

1940   Powell family moves to Hunts Point in the Bronx, a borough of New York City

1954   Graduates from Morris High School; enrolls in City College of New York (CCNY); joins the U.S. Army Reserve Officers Training Corps (ROTC)

1958   Graduates from CCNY at the top of his ROTC class; attends basic training and ranger schools

1959   Serves as a first lieutenant in West Germany

1960   Becomes a battalion adjutant at Fort Devens, Massachusetts

1962   Marries Alma Johnson; serves as advisor to an infantry battalion in Vietnam

1963   Son, Michael, is born; Powell is wounded in action in Vietnam and receives the Purple Heart

1965   Daughter Linda is born

1968	Graduates second in his class from the army's Command and General Staff College; promoted to division's assistant chief of staff in Vietnam
1969	Enrolls in George Washington University (GWU)
1971	Earns master of business administration degree from GWU; daughter Annemarie is born
1972	Powell is selected as White House Fellow; assigned to the Office of Management and Budget (OMB)
1973	Assumes command of the First Battalion in South Korea
1975	Enrolls in National War College
1976	Graduates with distinction from National War College
1977-78	Serves as executive to the special assistant to the secretary and deputy secretary of defense in President Jimmy Carter's administration
1979	Earns first general's star
1983	Serves as senior military assistant to the secretary of defense

1986	Becomes commander of the U.S. Army V Corps in Frankfurt, West Germany
1987	Becomes deputy national security advisor and then national security advisor
1989	Promoted to four-star general; appointed commander in chief of the U.S. Forces Command; becomes chairman of the Joint Chiefs of Staff (JCS); directs invasion of Panama to apprehend General Manuel Noriega
1990	Directs Operation Desert Shield in the Middle East
1991	Directs Operation Desert Storm in the Middle East; accepts a second term as JCS chairman
1993	Resigns position as JCS chairman
1995	Powell's autobiography, *My American Journey*, is published
1996	Delivers speech at the Republican National Convention in San Diego, California
1997	President Clinton names him General Chairman of The President's Summit for America's Future
2000	Delivers speech at the Republican National Convention in Philadelphia, Pennsylvania

Index

Melissa Banta has worked at Harvard for the past 12 years, where she serves as a curator of historic photographs and prints. She is the coauthor and coeditor of a number of publications and exhibitions, including "From Site to Site: Anthropology, Photography, and the Power of Imagery," "A Timely Encounter: Nineteenth-Century Photographs of Japan," and "The Invention of Photography and Its Impact on Learning." Banta received a bachelor of science degree in anthropology from the State University of New York at Buffalo and a master of science degree in communications from Boston University.

Picture Credits

AP/Wide World Photos: p. 42; Department of Defense, Still Media Records Center, U.S. Air Force: pp. 2 (Photo by Senior Airman Rodney Kerns), 65 (Photo by JO2 Joe Bartlett); The National Archives: pp. 33, 34; Colin Powell family album: pp. 14, 19, 22, 28, 39, 46; Reagan Presidential Library: p. 56; Reuters/Bettmann: pp. 6, 58, 69, 70; UPI/Bettmann: pp. 10, 51.